A Single Mother's Book of Devotions
30 - Days of Encouragement in The Word

Crystal S. Allen
Copyright ©2023 Crystal S. Allen

A
Single Mother's
Book of Devotions

30 - Days of Encouragement in the Word.

Crystal S. Allen
Copyright ©2023 Crystal S. Allen

A Single Mother's Book of Devotions
30 Days of Encouragement in the Word
Copyright ©2023 Crystal S. Allen
Published by Never A-Mis Enterprises, LLC
P.O. Box 2298
Byron, GA 31008-2298
www.neveramisenterprises.com

ISBN: 9798985059755

Printed in the United States of America

All rights reserved.
No part of this publication may be reproduced, stored in a retrieval system, or transmitted in any form or by any means - for example, electronic, photocopy, recording - without the prior written permission of the publisher. The only exception is brief quotations in printed reviews. The authorized purchaser has been granted a nontransferable, nonexclusive, and noncommercial right to

access and view this electronic publication, and purchaser agrees to do so only in accordance with the terms of use under which it was purchased or transmitted. Participation in or encouragement of piracy of copyrighted materials in violation of author's and publisher's right is prohibited.

KJV – *King James Version* Scripture taken from the King James Version. Authorized *King James Version – Public Domain*

NKJV – *New King James Version* ® copyright ©1982 by Thomas Nelson. Used by permission. All rights reserved.

AMP -*Amplified Version* Scripture copyright ©2015 by The Lockman Foundation, La Habra, CA 90631. All rights reserved.

NIV®- *New International Version* ®, copyright ©1973, 1978, 1984, 2011 by Biblica, Inc.® Used by permission. All rights reserved worldwide.

NLT – *New Living Translation*, copyright © 1996, 2004, 2015 by Tyndale House Foundation. Used by permission of Tyndale House Publishers, Inc., Carol Stream, Illinois 60188. All rights reserved.

ESV - *English Standard Version*, ® Text Edition: 2016. Copyright © 2001 by Crossway Bibles, a publishing ministry of Good News Publishers.

Merriam-Webster Online Dictionary copyright ©2021 by Merriam-Webster, Incorporated

Dedication

I dedicate this book of devotions to my three loving, Growing, and successful sons:

Zavian – Elijah – JaQuon.

They inspired me to write this book to inspire other single mothers of Faith.

Table of Content

Introduction

Day One – Pardon the Interruption!

Day Two - Take Cover.

Day Three – God's Intended Blessings.

Day Four – Be Anxious for Nothing!

Day Five – Fast Food ... A meal on the go.

Day Six – Ask and you shall receive.

Day Seven – Pray without ceasing.

Day Eight – Don't lose you, mother!

Day Nine – It's the 'JOY' for me.

Day Ten – No other choice but to trust You.

Day Eleven – The carrier.

Day Twelve – Priceless.

Day Thirteen – Promise keeper.

Day Fourteen – Powder room moment.

Day Fifteen – The Rock!

Day Sixteen – Co-parenting with wise counsel.

Day Seventeen – The unspoken.

Day Eighteen – As for me and my house, we will serve the Lord.

Day Nineteen – Spread thin ...

Day Twenty – The Example.

Day Twenty-One – Are you listening?

Day Twenty-Two – Be sober minded!

Day Twenty-Three – I prayed, now it's your turn.

Day Twenty-Four – Running on empty.

Day Twenty-Five – Damage control.

Day Twenty-Six – Strength from within.

Day Twenty-Seven – Remember when?

Day Twenty-Eight – Teach them the way!

Day Twenty-Nine – Attention!

Day Thirty – Jesus is The Head & the Boss!

Conclusion

About the Author

Introduction

This devotional journey I have embarked upon is meant to inspire and encourage you to recognize the blessings of each day; the beautiful life of a single mother of faith; how God has kept me grounded, while impacting my family with guided direction of God's Word. This devotional will also impact Spiritual mothers, Godmothers, grandmothers, and aunties to use, experience, and establish the cleansing power of The Word.

Being a single mother and the only partner in my home is The Lord, takes dedication and compassion. Most importantly, it takes commitment to be loyal to God and doing things His way. It can be very difficult, rewarding and fulfilling at the same time, producing teaching moments along the way. Every mother can relate to every fiber of their humanity being tested with some type of challenge.

As mothers, we are very busy, and it's easy to be overwhelmed, overlooked, outnumbered, and/or smothered by many different circumstances a day might hold. I am here to remind you of how gifted and strong you ARE! The beauty of being a Woman of purpose; chosen to bring forth life encased in unconditional love. We have been delicately created by God to walk in strength and stand in power. This Great blessing from God is also known as being a mother.

During this 30-day journey in the Word, I pray you will become intrigued to dig deeper. I pray you will allow my experiences become wisdom for your situation. Most importantly, I pray you will be awakened by the Great Refresher, Holy Spirit of God, in areas/ways you have been depleted!

LET'S BEGIN OUR 30-DAYS IN THE WORD.

DAY ONE

Pardon the Interruption!
Philippians 4:6-7 (NKJV)

Starting the day without a plan of action is a set-up for disaster. Since we have children, it is even more important to have a plan of action because we are responsible for more than just us! I write out my agenda, or I set reminders in my phone calendar to notify of something I need to do or where I need to be. Completing every task within my agenda would be lovely. The truth is some of us are hard on ourselves because we didn't finish everything that was on our list. We HAVE to give ourselves grace and extend ourselves a little mercy. The truth is I didn't get any time to myself because one of my kids had a crisis, we were able to overcome. Although I really needed the time for me, he needed me more.

I'm here to tell you that the unexpected interruptions are going to happen; but instead of getting frustrated, they're still a win. Extending ourselves grace and mercy will change how we view interruptions, distractions, and daily plans of actions! Being flexible is an invisible brace that will keep you grounded when one child is in crisis-mode, while the other child is just now telling you what he needs for the school field trip ... TOMORROW!

We shouldn't be anxious for anything. Take one step at time. This is a perfect place and opportunity to ask God for His help. It doesn't matter if you need His help for guidance. Or if you need His help for strength, He wants us to surrender our little agenda unto Him and let Him invade our space.

DAY TWO

Take cover!
Psalms 46:1-3 (MSG)

In the state of an emergency, our hearts will literally drop and panic, which causes unbelief to surface to the forefront. When everything becomes a blur, God steps in with His loving arms and gives us boldness to accept reality. The strength of God makes a mother rise up and stand as a strong warrior.

As a single mother, there have been countless times an emergency has broken out and I immediately went into survival/panic mode. After doing the former and seeing no hope in sight, I finally allowed God to step in and give me His strength and guidance. Instead of losing it, I accepted His strength to stop and purposely pray, coupled with fasting. Prayers of protection; healing and strength; praying without ceasing; sacrificing sleep and food; purposeful efforts of seeking to be in His presence, all became the actions of a Strong Warrior! The fearless warrior in us roars at the face of adversity and is purposed to be victorious. We know beyond a shadow of a doubt we are duplicating that which we have obtained from Abba Father; Who knows NO defeat. God covers us BY ANY MEANS NECESSARY!

DAY THREE

God's Intended Blessings.
James 2:14-26 (MSG)

As a single mother of Faith, I don't always know where money is going to come from my bills or to make sure the kids have what they need. I often tell the Lord, "God if You don't do it, it can't be done!" Even at that moment, a comfort and peace begin to overtake me because of no longer allowing worry, stress, and anxiety take residence in my mind. Unmasking the silent, loud thoughts in my mind has prepared layers to be peeled off so the strength of my faith could be utilized.

Now ... God can orchestrate the next

Move! Instead of worrying, I started praying; standing in the gap; encouraging myself and reminding myself of what He said; while waiting for Him to tell me what He wanted me to do. The place of wait became my place of peace because my perspective changed then my posture changed.

My posture change allowed me to hear God's instructions very clearly. I can remember Him saying, "Call this person." Sure enough, compassion was shown; the need was met, and pride was destroyed.

God showed me the bigger picture. When I stripped away my old mind-set, I was able to operate from a place of faith. Now I'm prepared to obtain INTENDED BLESSINGS!

DAY FOUR

Be anxious for *NOTHING*.
Matthew 26:41 (KJV

Where is my help? I'm tired and frustrated! STOP!!!! Don't worry. Pray. Remember God is and will remain faithful. In due season everything will fall in its correct place. Don't go before God, allow Him to lead.

I recall feeling ready for change, needing change, and mentally drained. In these times, I saturated my house with praise and worship music. Once I spent time with God, I was able to recharge and focus.

DAY FIVE

FAST food … A meal on the go.
Matthew 5:6 (MSG)

My teenage boys love to eat out no matter how much of a chef I think I am! The fast-food restaurants always have their revolving doors open welcoming us to spend our time and money satisfying our cravings. The Word of God is food for our soul. We can be greatly satisfied eating on God's Word.

The Word will fill and nourish us just like the restaurants can, but it will last longer and be better for our body, mind and soul. God's power in the Word will cause us to send up a praise because of the 'meal' prepared!

No matter how busy we get, remember we need a quick bite of the Word of God ... He that hungers and thirsts after righteousness shall be FILLED!

DAY SIX

Ask and you shall receive.
Matthew 7:7-8 (KJV)

As a child, I wanted to be a teacher. I didn't take the route I thought I would. As a mother, I lecture; plan; encourage; and teach. Raising children involves being a teacher and guiding them, while appreciating the hard work that comes along with it.

As I look back at my motherhood journey, I see great results; growth. My desire to become a teacher is being made a reality everyday as a mother. God wants us to depend on Him, knowing in faith we will receive the desires of our heart. We still have to ASK SO WE CAN RECEIVE!

DAY SEVEN

Pray without ceasing.
1 Thessalonians 5:16-18 (NLT)

Waking up feeling good; everything is in place for the day. No issues at work. Kids had a great day at school, no complaints. I'm so grateful for days like this; no worries, no stress.

Even though we have good days, and great days, we should STILL pray. We need to have constant prayer going forth; in an instant, things can go from GREAT too bad. There is always someone or something we can be praying or interceding for. Ask Holy Spirit to lead us into ALL truths so we can be found unselfishly praying WITHOUT CEASING!

DAY EIGHT

Don't lose you, mother!
Jeremiah 29:11 (NKJV)

Mother … Mom …Grandmother … Godmother … Auntie … Don't lose yourself. In the midst of motherhood, we are called with a Holy calling that we must be true to. Moving forward with the plans and purpose God has for our lives helps to stay the course and not get lost in our lives. A lot of times we put everything in front of our needs and our peace. We have to trust Him to lead and direct us as we travel down that path called motherhood.

If we ask the Lord to fill us up in the empty places, we can continue to walk in the fullness of who He has called us to be.

Instead of losing ourselves, we will gain SO MUCH MORE!

DAY NINE

It's the 'Joy' for me.
2 Corinthians 1:20 (NLT)

This joy that I have, the world didn't give it to me, and the world can't take away. We have to guard our heart, mind, and spirit. We have to hold on to every promise God has spoken in His Word. We are fearfully and wonderfully made. I am a Woman of God. I am a Mother of God. I am Beautiful. I am Strong. I AM FULL OF JOY!

[53]

DAY TEN

No other choice but to trust You.
Philippians 1:6 (KJV)

Lord, I trust the words that are echoed in my heart from You! My heart is surrendered to You, Lord. I have given my heart to many other things and many other people, but today giving my heart to You!

I trust You to hear my requests, petitions, and prayers concerning me and my children. Even though I think I know what's best for me; I trust You to give me what's best for me. I don't have any doubt You will not do exactly what You said You would do!

I don't have no other choice or option but to trust Him. He can't LIE!

DAY ELEVEN

The carrier.
Psalms 139:13-16 (KJV)

We're created spiritual beings specifically fashioned with a womb from a womb. The womb of a mother is a phenomenal, delicate design. The same way the baby is connected to us while in our womb is the same way we are connected to God. The connection for the baby to receive nutrients, blood, oxygen, and protection is the exact same way it is for us with God.

The sad part is most of us don't recognize who we are. We are carriers of Purpose and the Plans of God. We are carriers of nations, Kings and Queens.

The womb is the Greatest incubator there ever was. We need to remember how powerful our womb is and how powerful the WOMB of God IS and to our lives!

DAY TWELVE

Priceless.
Proverbs 31:30-31 (KJV)

We are queens! We are of a Royal Priesthood. God has given His people authority to speak a thing. His promises are "Yes" and "Amen".

We are priceless vessels. There is not a situation or circumstance that should cause us to forget who we are and what we deserve. Don't panic … you got this! We have to make our request made known unto the King of all Kings.

Remember, we have been given the authority to speak; we have to make sure we are walking as royalty. We are priceless vessels. SPEAK LIFE!

DAY THIRTEEN

Promise keeper!
Habakkuk 2:1-3 (KJV)

God is a Promise Keeper! What God has spoken … What He has declared for our family … What He has declared for us … We have to see it through His eyes.

We have to write the vison and make it plain so our children can read it and run with it. Let's teach our kids to dream big and write the vision.

Midnight miracles come in all shapes and sizes!

DAY FOURTEEN

Powder room moment!
Proverbs 31:28-29 (KJV)

Slowing down to be still is often a place/state is often spoken of, but rarely done. In desperation of right now manifestations or results, waiting, being still or slowing down is not the first thought.

It seems as though we are always on the Potter's wheel; more like the mouse's wheel; running fast and going nowhere! Unfortunately, anything worth having is worth waiting for. Instead of getting frustrated on how long the process is taking, change your focus. Sis, you have been able to make it through some things you NEVER dreamed you would.

Stop! Take a moment to freshen up and powder your nose. Exhale. Regroup! Now that you have re-focused, before you know it, our children will rise up and called us blessed!

DAY FIFTEEN

The Rock!
2 Samuel 22:2 (KJV)

Our foundation is built on the Cornerstone called Jesus. He is our Rock of Gibraltar. Our Sure foundation.

Because of The Rock we can shake off things quickly. We can recover quickly. We can withstand the storms of life and still smile. The Rock is more than solid, He is protection and safety.

The Rock will render us a SOLID!

DAY SIXTEEN

Co-Parenting with Wise Counsel.
Proverbs 19:20-21 (KJV)

Thank You, Lord, I can always count on You to help with making decisions. There are times when we need Him to help us make decisions others may never understand. He is dependable and available whenever we need Him.

As Believers there is a certain standard in which we live and maintain. The standard protects us from open access to just anybody. Monthly, daily, or hourly, He is ready to help us.

Every open access to The Holy Spirit will fill every void; answer questions; and gives Him the opportunity to boldly step in and minister to us, while nurturing us at the same time.

When we seek Wise Counsel, we will NOT be disappointed!

DAY SEVENTEEN

The unspoken.
Ephesians 6:18 (NIV)

Sometimes as mothers, we can be so overwhelmed with concern, for our kids will begin to experience what we're dealing with. Our kids have a lot they are already dealing with; and then unknowingly taking on our burdens can be very difficult and overwhelming for them.

Communication is not only verbalizing one's heart, but it also releases and directs prayer. Unfortunately, we will not always know what our kids are thinking, but God knows. He knows what we can't or are unwilling to know.

Prayer is the key to unlock the unspoken. We have to be confident in God and trust He will reveal all that concerns us and our kids ... even the UNSPOKEN!

DAY EIGHTEEN

As for me and my house, we will serve The Lord.
Proverbs 22:6 (KJV)

Children aren't always enthusiastic about going to church. Why? Funny thing is I was the same way and back then I didn't have a reason. My parents overrode what I wanted, and instilled morals and values in me. It's my responsibility to do the same with my boys.

We have to educate them with the truth of Who Really wakes them up every morning; Who provides the breath we breath; and Who protects us from dangers seen and unseen.

Our lifestyle is our worship. Our testimonies teach us. Our children should see the Christ in us at home as well as the same Christ when we go to church.

DAY NINETEEN

Spread thin …
Psalms 55:22 (AMP)

We can't be in more than one place at one time! I have three boys that have different personalities; different activities; and different interests, or better known as a juggling act! Some single mothers have more and some have less, either way it only takes a second to become overwhelmed and worn thin. When we realize we are being spread thin, it is imperative that we find a space or a place to allow God to refuel us.

My secret place: my refueling station is where I am able to release frustration, fears, doubts, and the weight of the world that weighs down on me. My secret place is also my safe place!

DAY TWENTY

The example.

John 13:15 (AMP)

When we hear people say "These are definitely your kids! There is no denying that!" Those types of comments stir up a sense of pride because we want our kids to have great character, be respectful, exercise good hyenine and so on; exhibiting what we have as parents have had the opportunity to instill in them.

We are infamous for telling our kids, "Have respect. Mind your manners, or act like you have some sense!" The same paraphrased words are in the Bible because these instructions are not limited to children.

We are examples to our kids; Christ is our Example. He is the Greatest Example … We are Christians, we should have CHRIST- LIKE characteristics and qualities.

DAY TWENTY-ONE

Are you listening?

James 1:19(KJV)

What has captured your attention so much so you can't focus on what you're doing? In life, we encounter many different distractions; no matter your age; children or no children; married or single, we have to pay attention to what we are listening to.

Paying more attention to what we are allowing to take our focus will cause us to be more intentional with our listening. From social media to television, we can waste so much time doing nothing! Renewing our minds daily will help us to declutter and evict unnecessary thoughts, imaginations, and 'should a- would a' residing in our minds where the Word of God; goal setting, and maturing should be.

I wish I would have utilized my time and listened to instructions back then. If you are like me and look back to see the mistakes made and opportunities missed, let me help you. STOP IT!! Someone told me that looking back only sets me up to collide with what is in front of me. Remember Lot's wife. The past is a paid for ticket into our future. Whatever lesson we learned, we paid for it some kind of way!

DAY TWENTY-TWO

Be sober minded!

1Peter 5:8 (KJV)

As a mother of multiple children, I do my best to ensure their safety. I don't have the luxury of being spiritic and impulsive. I can't be everywhere they are at the same time, so I have Great assurance my Father God in heaven watches over us all. While God does His part, we have to make sure we are going our part; being leveled headed or sober minded, helps so we can be watchful for what we don't see, and utilize discernment for what we can't see.

I have learned each one of my son's behaviors and personalities. Being sober minded has allowed me to think before responding to some of things they may do or say. Being levelheaded/sober minded put a roadblock in place to stop a lot of unnecessary issues taking place.

DAY TWENTY-THREE

I prayed, now it's your turn.

Proverbs 22:6 (KJV)

As single mothers of Faith, we have a due diligence to pray and intercede for your children, first. They have to see us praying with their *own* eyes and/or hear us with their *own* ears! The example we set at home should be spilling out into other areas/places we frequent. After we have consistently taken them to church, nurtured them in the Word, and instilled morals, principles, and values; what's next?

I'm glad you asked what was next! The 'next' is them reciprocating by praying themselves. They saw and heard me praying, so they have an idea of how its' done, except they can pray in their own way. They can pray at school when their anxiety starts to elevate. They can pray at a game and ask Father God to protect everyone. Because of the example I am at home, they now have to the tools to be an example and pray wherever they are!

DAY TWENTY-FOUR

Running on an empty tank.
Jeremiah 29:11 (KJV)

Days turn into weeks, and weeks turn into months of pouring out; giving to others; or waiting on some type of good news, begins to wear very thin. These times are not only disheartening, but they can set one up for disparaging disappointment. Seemingly no hope is in sight!

These are times I've only had the promise (s) in God's Word that gave me peace in KNOWING … If the thoughts He thinks of me are only a thought; I can allow it to strengthen me until the 'thought' becomes reality!

Let the weak same I am strong!

Trouble don't last always.

DAY TWENTY-FIVE

Damage control.
Colossians 3:12 (KJV)

Even though we teach our kids to be kind and manurable, misunderstandings can still happen. Building relationships takes time. We can have the purest intentions, and things can still be perceived wrong.

In the midst of a misunderstanding while building, we can't throw away the work and effort that has already been exhausted. This is the time to access the damage and then do damage control. Learn those who labor and build with you. I pray you will be able to discern people's motive, so you won't feel like all of your labor is in vain when building healthy, lasting relationships. Damage control is not a bad thing, it is a NEEDFUL thing!

DAY TWENTY-SIX

Strength from within.
Ephesians 3:16-20 (NIV)

Our children are facing situations they shouldn't be facing as middle or high schoolers. Listening to my boys talk about pressures, stressors, and bullying lets me know they are not exempt from being attacked by the enemy, even though they are children! There are both good and bad peer pressures; tasks of fitting in while trying to find out who they are is a constant fight. While our kids are fighting forces outside of the home, they are still battling with what to do with what we are teaching them inside the home. Single parent homes are catching it just as well as two-parent homes. There is a constant battle in their head; right or wrong; good or bad.

As a parent of Faith, we must with doing things according to the Bible … Period! As we continually pray and are students of the Word, what we need, when we need it will come forth. Not just what we need, but above and beyond what we need. We are making substantial deposits so we can make even more substantial withdrawals!

DAY TWENTY-SEVEN

Remember when?

Ephesians 2:4-5 (KJV)

Every now and then we look back to see where we have come from! We look back and we're able to see the pits, traps, and caves He pulled and saved us from! I wouldn't have known what a miracle looked like until I saw Him move in my life and do things ONLY He could do!

Looking back and remembering only becomes dangerous when we're trying to relive that moment with regrets. Just remember where you were instead of trying to remember why!

DAY TWENTY-EIGHT

Teach them the way.

Deuteronomy 6:6-7 (ESV)

In obedience to God, we teach our kids the way. A teacher studies so as to be able to distribute the information in different ways so the student has the capacity to learn it at the level they are on. As mothers, we are forever learning how to best teach our kids so they can receive and retain the information. The Holy Spirit will teach us how to teach our children individually and collectively.

Just like students, or kids have different personalities; different learning skills; are on different levels of understanding. If we allow Holy Spirit to help us, we can't go wrong. The teaching will be so simple that not even a little child can error.

DAY TWENTY-NINE

ATTENTION!
Proverbs 29:17-19 (NIV)

What are you doing that captivates you? What are you doing that distracts you? Are you focused and task driven? Whether captivated or distracted, we have to be mindful of what is keeping us from getting to a place; moving out of a place, or keeping us in a place we shouldn't be.

Our children grow up quickly. We don't have time to be stuck in a place too long. We need to have razor focus; wisely investing our attention in people, places, and things ordained by God. Only what we do for Christ matters.

Lastly, when our attention is not where it's supposed to be, we become vulnerable and open to the enemy's ploys to distract us from the will, plan, and purpose of God for our lives, our children's lives, and everyone else connected to us.

ATTENTION! ATTENTION! ATTENTION!

DAY THIRTY

Jesus is The Head & The Boss!

1 Corinthians 11:1-3 (KJV)

We believe God has given us the blueprint and lessen plan on how to teach and guide our kids, we have to formulate some of thoughts like a business. He is teaching and training us, so we can teach and train them.

We run a business in our households, and our children are the employees. Some of their wages earned may not pay out when the work is done, but eventually the pay-out will greater than they could have imagined.

We are delegating tasks; giving lectures; writing them up when something is not done and teaching them the business trade of life. We set the standard. Have we raised the bar and given them something to reach for?

Life is what you make it; and so is your business and your employees!

CONCLUSION

As a single mother of three, I have grown to the place of continuous worship and constant devotion to keep myself encouraged. My mistakes have taught me valuable lessons, while Holy Spirit refills me with courage to move on and try again.

My purpose is to encourage both mother and child. If the mother is encouraged, she will most definitely love on the child. Someone else's thought can trigger our mind and thoughts. I don't have all the answers, and my way may not be the best way. If we continue to rely on the

Lord, we will receive the BEST answer for us and our children.

In closing, please receive this gift of encouragement wrapped in love!

Your sister in Christ & Mother of Faith,

Sis Crystal.

THE BIO

CRYSTAL S. ALLEN

Crystal Shata' Allen is the daughter of Geraldine Allen & late Robert L Allen Jr. Crystal has 3 siblings. Lady Allen was born in Milledgeville, Ga and raised in Jones County. She graduated from Jones Co High School. Lady Allen graduated from Central GA Technology with a diploma in College in Health Technology; and a graduate of SNHU with a B.A. in Liberal Arts and General Studies.

Lady Crystal Allen is a loving and strong single mother to her three son's: Zavian 20, Jaquon 19, and Elijah 18, who are her heart and inspiration for this book. Lady Allen currently resides in Macon Georgia

Lady Crystal Allen serves under the Leadership of Bishop Robert Knight Jr and the late Overseer Willie Frazier at Kingdom Shift Apostolic Church in Milledgeville, GA as Praise Leader & Minister of Music.

Lady Crystal enjoys cooking and creating with her hands. She also likes to create self-made catering dishes in her spare time.

www.ingramcontent.com/pod-product-compliance
Lightning Source LLC
LaVergne TN
LVHW021355080426
835508LV00020B/2285